Franklin School
Summit Public Schools

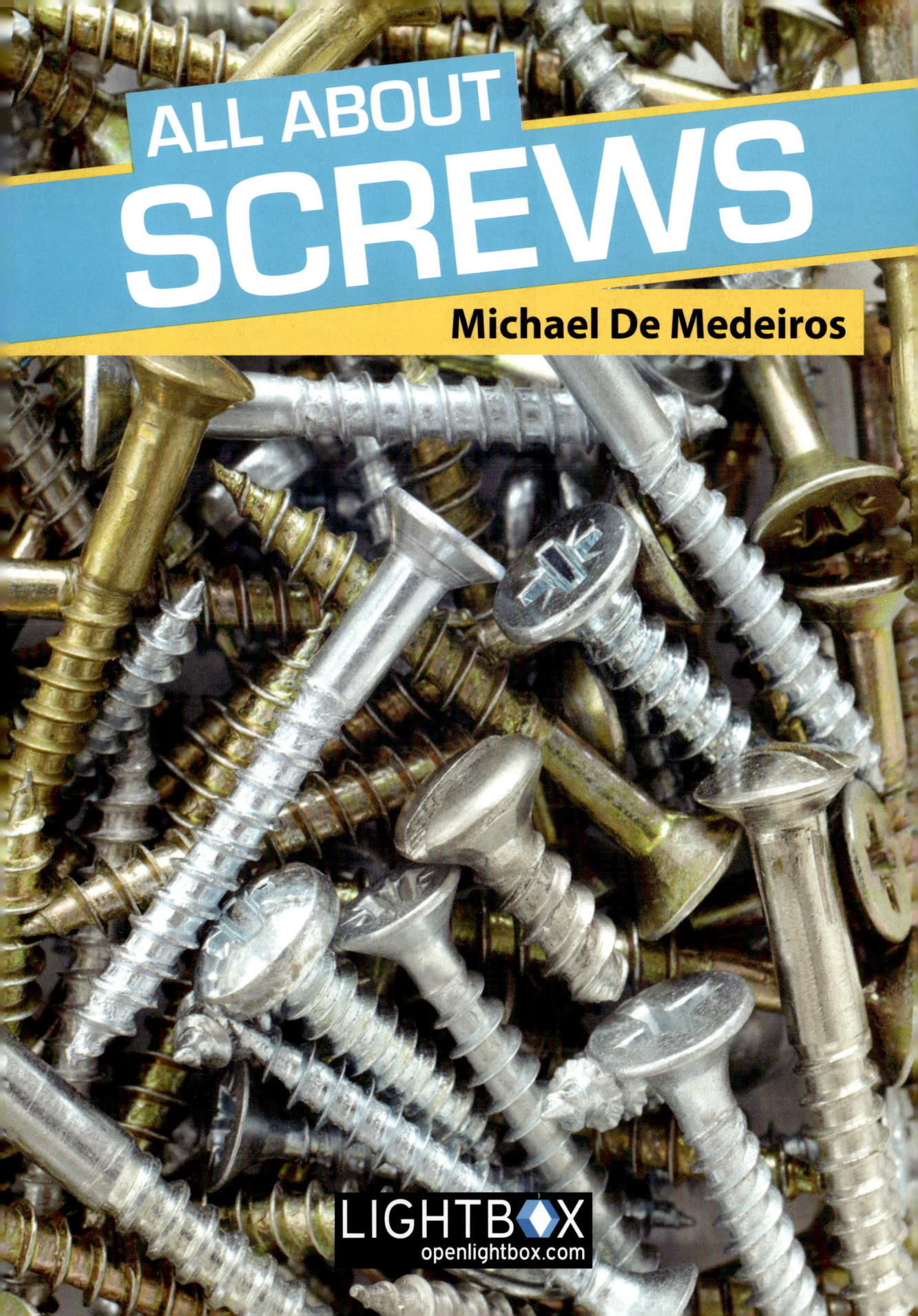

ALL ABOUT
SCREWS

Michael De Medeiros

LIGHTBOX
openlightbox.com

Go to
www.openlightbox.com
and enter this book's
unique code.

ACCESS CODE

LBG23668

Lightbox is an all-inclusive digital solution for the teaching and learning of curriculum topics in an original, groundbreaking way. Lightbox is based on National Curriculum Standards.

STANDARD FEATURES OF LIGHTBOX

AUDIO High-quality narration using text-to-speech system

ACTIVITIES Printable PDFs that can be emailed and graded

SLIDESHOWS Pictorial overviews of key concepts

VIDEOS Embedded high-definition video clips

WEBLINKS Curated links to external, child-safe resources

TRANSPARENCIES Step-by-step layering of maps, diagrams, charts, and timelines

INTERACTIVE MAPS Interactive maps and aerial satellite imagery

QUIZZES Ten multiple choice questions that are automatically graded and emailed for teacher assessment

KEY WORDS Matching key concepts to their definitions

Copyright © 2017 Smartbook Media Inc. All rights reserved.

CONTENTS

Lightbox Access Code................... 2

The Screw.. 4

Simple Machines 6

Using Screws 8

Screws of the World 10

Ancient Screws............................. 12

Screws Timeline 13

Force and Movement................. 14

Working with Force 16

How Screws Work........................ 18

What Is a
Hydraulic Engineer? 20

Brain Teasers 21

Screws in Action........................... 22

Key Words/Index.......................... 23

Log on to
www.openlightbox.com............ 24

All About Screws

The Screw

Screws are rods with sharp edges called threads. These threads form a spiral around the outside of the rod. The threads make it easier for a screw to move through a substance, such as metal, stone, or wood. People use screws in many different ways. Screws fasten objects together. They may also be used to move something from one height to another. Spiral staircases are shaped like screws. Screws such as **propellers** may push water or air.

The screw is a type of simple machine. A machine is a device that uses power to do a task. There are six kinds of simple machines. They are the inclined plane, the lever, the pulley, the screw, the wedge, and the wheel and axle. Simple machines make **work** easier, but they do not add **energy** of their own. Instead, simple machines change the **effort** needed to perform tasks.

Threads make screws **300 times** stronger than nails for holding objects together.

The oldest spiral staircase that still exists is **2,500 years old**. It stands in Selinunte, Sicily.

The world's largest ship propeller blades are **34 feet long**. (10.5 meters)

Simple Machines

Spiral staircases make climbing stairs easier because they spread out the climber's effort over a longer distance.

All About Screws

Simple Machines

The inclined plane and the lever are the most basic of all simple machines. They can even be found in other types of simple machines.

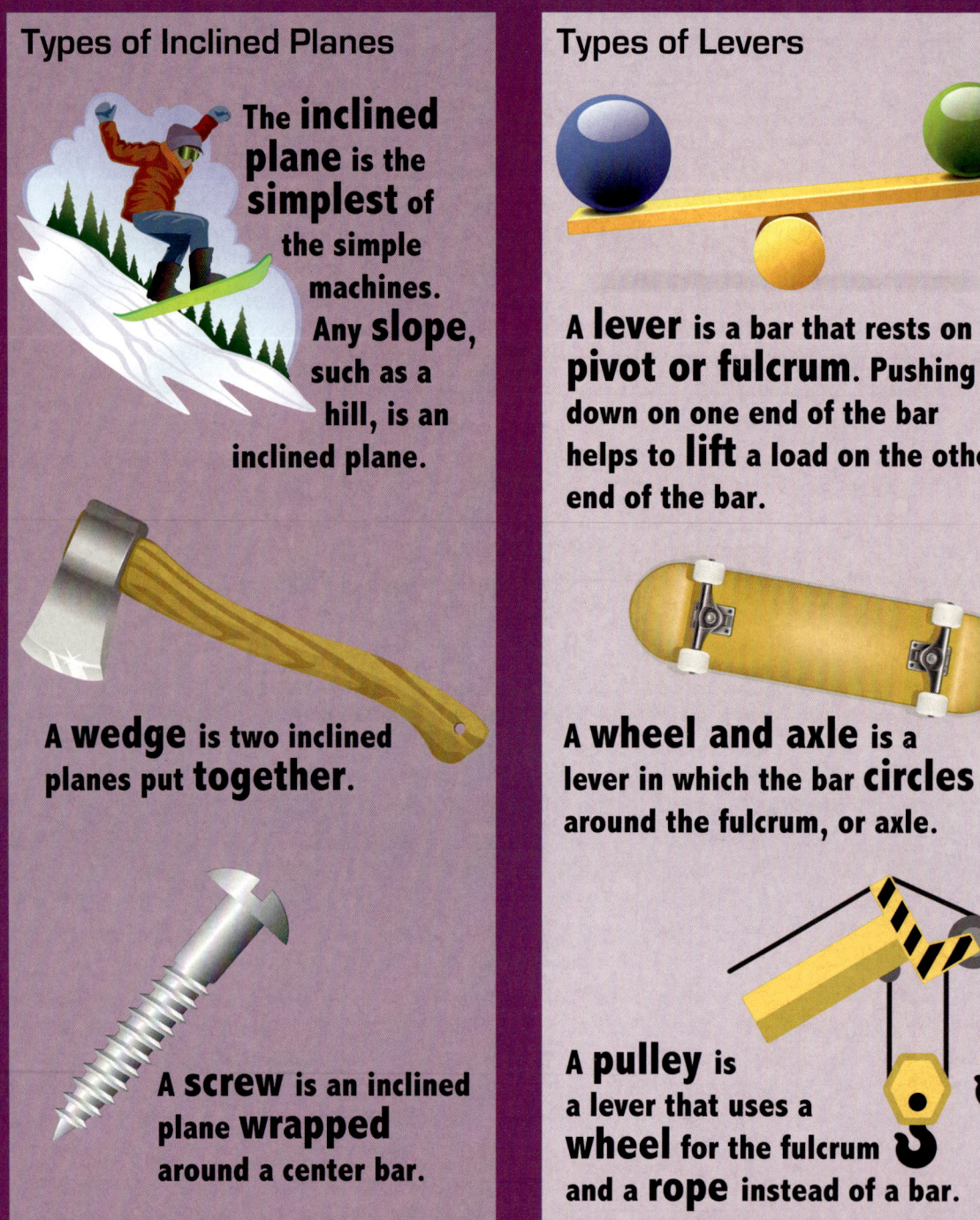

Types of Inclined Planes

The **inclined plane** is the **simplest** of the simple machines. Any **slope**, such as a hill, is an inclined plane.

A **wedge** is two inclined planes put **together**.

A **screw** is an inclined plane **wrapped** around a center bar.

Types of Levers

A **lever** is a bar that rests on a **pivot or fulcrum**. Pushing down on one end of the bar helps to **lift** a load on the other end of the bar.

A **wheel and axle** is a lever in which the bar **circles** around the fulcrum, or axle.

A **pulley** is a lever that uses a **wheel** for the fulcrum and a **rope** instead of a bar.

From Simple to Complex

Simple machines can be combined to make other kinds of machines. When simple machines are combined, the new device is often called a compound or complex machine. Screws can be used together with other simple machines to create many useful devices.

Electric Drill
The drill's bit, or part that enters a surface, is a screw. An electric motor turns a wheel and axle, making the drill bit spin.

Eyeglasses
Small screws hold the frames of eyeglasses together. The hinges where the sides meet the front piece act as levers. The nose pads are wedges, holding the glasses on the face.

Car Jack
Wheels help a car jack slide into place under the car. A lever is used to lift the car off the ground. Screws hold the parts of the jack together.

All About Screws

Using Screws

Screws have been used for thousands of years. In ancient times, people used them to move water or to press the juice from grapes. During the 1400s, people in Europe began using metal screws to join objects together.

Today, screws are still used for all of these purposes. They are also used in faucets so that another object, such as a filter or hose, can be attached to the faucet. A type of screw without a pointed end is called a bolt. It is often used to hold parts together in large machines and structures.

Modern machines use large, screw-shaped devices to help squeeze the juice out of grapes.

Screws at Work

People all around the world use screws every day.

Auger
An auger is a type of screw that is used to make holes. There are different kinds of augers for digging holes in soil, ice, or wood. Some augers are used to make holes in leather.

Worm Gear
Worm **gears** are shaped like screws. When the worm gear turns, its teeth move a gear that is connected to it. Many types of factory machinery use worm gears.

Vice
A vice is a tool in which a screw tightens or loosens the grip on an object. Vices hold objects in place, such as a piece of wood to be cut or two objects that are being glued.

Nuts and Bolts
Bolts cannot create a hole in an object. The hole has to be drilled first. Bolts are useful for joining two objects. Nuts fit onto the bolts to hold the objects firmly together.

All About Screws

Screws of the World

People in many different cultures use screws to make their work easier. For more than 1,500 years, farmers in southern Europe and the Middle East have been using screws in olive presses, which squeeze the oil out of olives. Screws are also used in the latest farming equipment.

NETHERLANDS In 2014, a company in Rotterdam created a new kind of wind turbine for producing electricity. The device is shaped like a screw, allowing it to catch and use more wind than earlier types of turbines.

CHILE In 2010, a mine in the Atacama Desert collapsed, trapping 33 miners. Three huge drills were brought to the site to dig tunnels to reach the miners. After 69 days, the men were rescued.

NORTH AMERICA

ATLANTIC OCEAN

PACIFIC OCEAN

SOUTH AMERICA

0 2,000 Kilometers
0 1,000 Miles

Simple Machines

Digging machines at mines rely on screws. Screw-shaped devices are helping to produce energy. This map shows places where screws are very useful.

3

BELGIUM The largest combine harvesters in the world are made in Zedelgem. A blade in the front of the vehicle cuts wheat. A spinning screw pushes the wheat toward the vehicle's center.

4

CHINA The world's longest spiral staircase winds up the Canton Tower in Guangzhou. The staircase has more than 1,000 steps.

All About Screws 11

Ancient Screws

During the third century BC, Greek scientist Archimedes developed a machine for raising water. He put one end of a large screw inside a pipe and placed the pipe in water. As a person turned the screw with a handle, water was trapped between the threads and pushed up the pipe. This invention, called the Archimedes screw, is still used in many ways today. In some countries, farmers bring water to their crops with the device.

For centuries, the Archimedes screw was also used to keep ships from sinking. For example, if a ship ran into a sharp rock, the rock could tear a hole in the hull, or bottom part, of the ship. Water could then fill the hull, causing the ship to sink. The Archimedes screw was used to pull water out of the hull, keeping the ship afloat.

After a few turns of an Archimedes screw, water pours out of the top of the device.

Screws Timeline

600s BC
Devices similar to the Archimedes screw may have been used to bring water to the Hanging Gardens of Babylon in the Middle East.

About AD 50
Greek mathematician Heron of Alexandria lists the screw as one of the five simple machines he describes.

1400s
The screwdriver is invented, making it easier for workers to turn screws.

1680s
Corkscrews are used to open bottles sealed with a cork.

1797
Henry Maudslay invents a machine that makes evenly sized screws.

1487
Italian artist and inventor Leonardo da Vinci designs the airscrew. This machine uses a spinning screw to lift it off the ground like a helicopter.

1839
The *Archimedes* is the first ship to use a screw propeller.

1999
Scientist John Burland of Great Britain uses devices with Archimedes screws to help make the Leaning Tower of Pisa in Italy more stable.

1908
Businessman P. L. Robertson of Canada invents a screw with a square opening on top for the screwdriver. The design makes the screwdriver less likely to slip and cause injury.

All About Screws

When a child blows on a pinwheel, the force of his or her breath pushes the pinwheel's blades.

Force and Movement

Force is a push or a pull that causes an object to move or change its direction. When an object is not moving, or is at rest, all of the forces pushing or pulling on it are balanced. This balance is called equilibrium.

When scientists study forces and how objects move, there are three important measurements they take into account. They figure out an object's weight, how fast it is moving, and the amount of force that is causing the object to move. Understanding forces, how forces affect objects, and how objects affect each other can make it easier to move objects.

Understanding Gravity

Gravity is a force that pulls objects toward one another. All objects have some gravity, but it is often weak. An object's gravity is related to its **mass**. The more mass an object has, the greater its force of gravity. Earth is huge and has a great deal of mass. As a result, it has strong gravity that pulls objects toward the center of the planet.

Earth's gravity gives weight to the objects on its surface. How much an object weighs on Earth depends on the amount of mass it has. For example, a bowling ball has more mass than a rubber ball the same size, so the bowling ball weighs more on Earth.

Mass vs. Weight

Sometimes, people think that mass and weight are the same thing. However, this is not the case. An object's mass is always the same. Its weight can change depending on where the object is located.

Mass is usually measured in kilograms (kg), while weight is often measured in pounds. A person with a mass of 91 kilograms weighs 200 pounds on Earth. This is because Earth's gravity pulls on a 91-kilogram mass with a force of 200 pounds. The Moon has much weaker gravity, so the same person weighs less there. The Moon's gravity pulls on a 91-kilogram mass with a force of only 33 pounds. That same person has almost no weight on a spacecraft because there is little gravity. He or she weighs about 0 pounds, even though the person's mass is still 91 kilograms.

All About Screws

Working with Force

In science, work happens when a force is used to move an object over a distance. For work to happen, the force must be applied in the same direction that the object is moving. For example, lifting a rock off the ground is work. The force applied to pull the rock up is going in the same upward direction that the rock is moving.

Work also happens when a person pushes a rock forward along the ground. However, pushing against a very heavy rock and failing to move it is not work. The person may feel tired from his or her effort. Yet, if the rock has not moved, no work has taken place.

A great deal of force has to be applied to push a large bale of hay forward.

As the force needed to move an object increases, the work involved in moving it increases as well. This also applies to distance. The amount of work needed to move an object increases as the distance the object must move increases.

Simple machines make doing work easier. They do this by changing the amount and the direction of the force needed to move an object. Although less force is needed, simple machines require moving a greater distance.

Calculating Work

The amount of work needed to lift a 10-pound (4.5-kg) ball changes based on the distance it is lifted. To calculate the work, the weight of the ball is multiplied by the height it will be moved.

10 x 2 = 20

It takes 20 pounds (9.1 kg) of effort to lift the ball 2 feet (0.6 m).

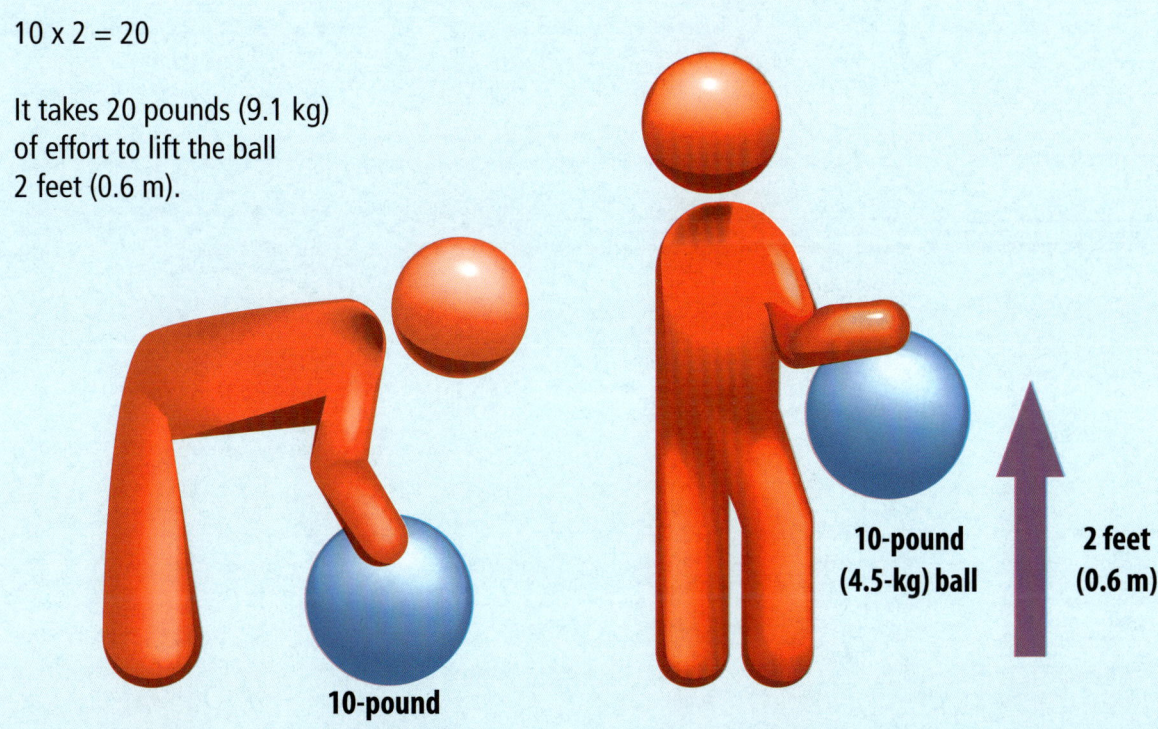

10-pound (4.5-kg) ball

10-pound (4.5-kg) ball

2 feet (0.6 m)

All About Screws

> The threads on a screw increase the force that is applied to move the screw into an object.

How Screws Work

Screws make work easier because they offer a **mechanical advantage**. When a person turns a screwdriver to put a screw into a block of wood, the threads on the screw change the twisting motion into forward movement. The mechanical advantage comes from the fact that it takes less force to turn the screwdriver than it would to push the screw straight into the wood.

Friction is also helpful when using screws. Screws are often used to hold wooden furniture together. Friction between the wood and each of the threads on all of the screws strongly holds the screws in place. This gives screws an advantage over nails. Nails do not have threads, so there is less friction holding them in place. Over time, nails are more likely to come loose than screws.

Simple Machines

Calculating Effort

The mechanical advantage of a screw depends on the number of threads it has. More threads means less force must be applied to the screwdriver. However, the screwdriver must be turned more and move a greater distance. A screw with fewer threads means the screwdriver makes fewer turns and moves less total distance. However, more force must be applied to each twist.

Screw C has the fewest threads. It will need the most force to turn. However, it will take fewer turns of the screwdriver to finish putting in screw C than it will for screws A or B.

Screw B has fewer threads, so more force will be needed to turn it than screw A.

Screw A is the easiest to turn because it has the most threads.

All About Screws

What Is a Hydraulic Engineer?

Hydraulic **engineers** study liquids such as water, and they design devices that use or move liquids. They may design dams to help supply cities with water. Hydraulic engineers study math and science in college, and they often receive advanced degrees. They use their skills to create many useful devices.

Hydraulic engineers in the Netherlands developed water screws powered by electricity to move water away from land at risk for flooding.

Henry F. Phillips

Henry F. Phillips was born in 1890 in Portland, Oregon. In 1933, he started the Phillips Screw Company. Phillips saw a need in the car industry for screws that would not come loose. He invented a new kind of screw with X-shaped grooves in the head for the screwdriver. This head allowed the screw to be tightened and not twist out of shape. By 1940, more than 85 percent of companies that made screws in the United States were using his design.

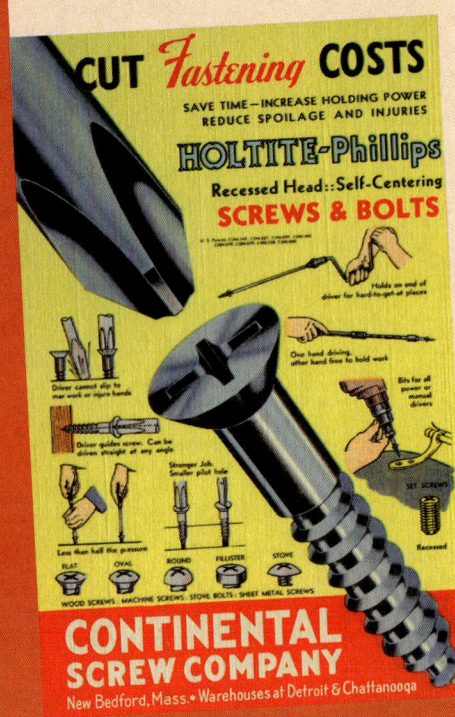

Brain Teasers

1 What is a screw?

2 What is an auger?

3 What is a bolt?

4 Who invented a machine for raising water in the third century BC?

5 What are the six kinds of simple machines?

6 How do simple machines make doing work easier?

7 What do hydraulic engineers design?

8 When did metal screws begin to be used to fasten objects together?

9 Which has stronger gravity, Earth or the Moon?

10 Who invented a machine in 1797 to make evenly sized screws?

ANSWERS: 1. A screw is a rod with sharp edges called threads spiraling around it. 2. An auger is a type of screw used to make holes. 3. A bolt is a screw without a pointed end. 4. Archimedes invented the device now called the Archimedes screw. 5. The six kinds of simple machines are the inclined plane, the lever, the pulley, the screw, the wedge, and the wheel and axle. 6. Simple machines change the amount and direction of the force needed to move an object. 7. Hydraulic engineers design devices that use or move liquids. 8. Metal screws began to be used in the 1400s. 9. Earth has stronger gravity than the Moon. 10. Henry Maudslay invented a machine to make evenly sized screws.

All About Screws

Screws in Action

Learn more about how screws help people use less force but over a greater distance to perform a task.

Materials Needed

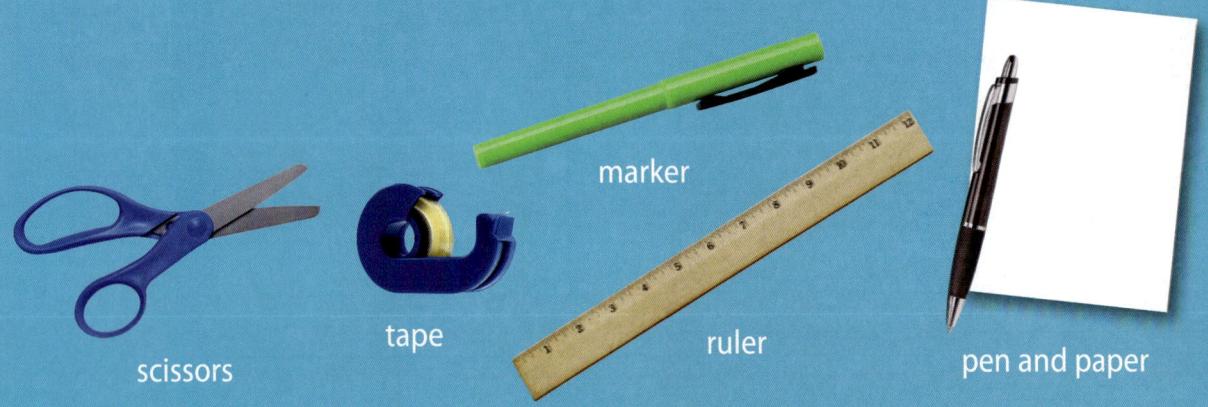

scissors   tape   marker   ruler   pen and paper

Directions

1 Use the ruler to draw a triangle on the paper. Be sure the triangle has one **right angle**.

2 Cut out the triangle with the scissors.

3 With the marker, draw a line along the longest edge of the triangle.

4 Attach the shortest side of the triangle to the pen with a piece of tape.

5 Wrap the triangle tightly around the pen. Observe the shape of the line you drew when you have wrapped the triangle all the way around the pen. See how much longer the line is than the length of the pen.

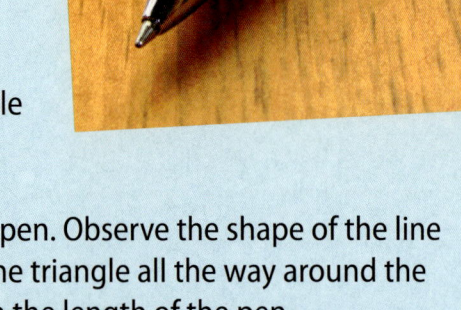

Simple Machines

Key Words

effort: the power being used to move something

energy: the power needed to do work

engineers: people who use science to solve practical problems

friction: a gripping force that is created when two objects come in contact with each other

gears: wheels with teeth around the edges that fit together

mass: a measure of the amount of material an object contains

mechanical advantage: a measure of how much easier a task is made when a simple machine is used

propellers: devices that spin to move a boat forward through the water or a plane through the air

right angle: the corner of a square formed where two lines meet

work: power applied over distance to move an object

Index

Archimedes screws 12, 13, 21
augers 9, 21

blades 4, 11, 14
bolts 8, 9, 21

Canton Tower 11
car jacks 7
combine harvesters 11
complex machines 7
compound machines 7

distance 5, 16, 17, 19, 22
drills 7, 9, 10

effort 4, 5, 16, 17, 19
energy 4, 11
equilibrium 14
eyeglasses 7

forces 14, 15, 16, 17, 18, 19, 21, 22
friction 18

gravity 15, 21

hydraulic engineers 20, 21

inclined planes 4, 6

Leonardo da Vinci 13
levers 4, 6, 7

mass 15
mechanical advantage 18, 19

Phillips, Henry F. 20
propellers 4, 13
pulleys 4, 6

right angle 22

screwdrivers 13, 18, 19, 20
ships 4, 12
spiral staircases 4, 5, 11,

threads 4, 8, 12, 18, 19, 21
turbines 10

vices 9

wedges 4, 6, 7
weight 14, 15, 17
wheels and axles 4, 6, 7
work 4, 9, 10, 16, 17, 18, 21
worm gears 9

All About Screws

SUPPLEMENTARY RESOURCES

Click on the plus icon ⊕ found in the bottom left corner of each spread to open additional teacher resources.

- Download and print the book's quizzes and activities
- Access curriculum correlations
- Explore additional web applications that enhance the Lightbox experience

LIGHTBOX DIGITAL TITLES
Packed full of integrated media

VIDEOS

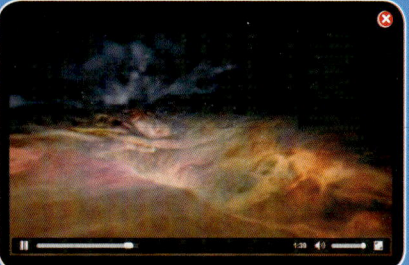

INTERACTIVE MAPS

WEBLINKS

SLIDESHOWS

QUIZZES

OPTIMIZED FOR
✓ TABLETS
✓ WHITEBOARDS
✓ COMPUTERS
✓ AND MUCH MORE!

Published by Smartbook Media Inc.
350 5th Avenue, 59th Floor
New York, NY 10118
Website: www.openlightbox.com

Copyright © 2017 Smartbook Media Inc. All rights reserved. No part of this publication may be reproduced, stored in a retrieval system, or transmitted in any form or by any means, electronic, mechanical, photocopying, recording, or otherwise, without the prior written permission of the publisher.

Library of Congress Control Number: 2016935459

ISBN 978-1-5105-0957-3 (hardcover)
ISBN 978-1-5105-0959-7 (multi-user eBook)

Printed in Brainerd, Minnesota, United States
1 2 3 4 5 6 7 8 9 0 20 19 18 17 16

032016
090316

Project Coordinator Heather Kissock
Art Director Terry Paulhus

Photo Credits
Every reasonable effort has been made to trace ownership and to obtain permission to reprint copyright material. The publisher would be pleased to have any errors or omissions brought to its attention so that they may be corrected in subsequent printings. The publisher acknowledges Getty Images, Corbis, Alamy, Shutterstock, and iStock as its primary image suppliers for this title.